Hansel and Gretel

Level 3

Retold by Cameron Fox

Series Editor: Melanie Williams

Pearson Education Limited
Pearson
KAO Two
KAO Park
Harlow
Essex
CM17 9NA

and Associated Companies throughout the world.

ISBN 9781292240077

First published by Librairie du Liban Publishers, 1996
This adaptation first published by
Penguin Books 2000
3 5 7 9 10 8 6 4
Text copyright © Pearson Education Limited 2000
Illustrations copyright © 1996 Librairie du Liban

Retold by Cameron Fox
Series Editor: Melanie Williams
Designed by Shireen Nathoo Design
Illustrated by Claire Mumford

Printed in China
SWTC/03

The moral right of the author and illustrator have been asserted

Published by Pearson Education Limited

For a complete list of titles available in the Pearson Story Readers series please write
to your local Pearson Education office or contact:
Pearson, KAO Two, KAO Park, Harlow, Essex, CM17 9NA

Answers for the Activities in this book are published in the free Pearson English Story
Readers Factsheet on the website, www.pearsonenglishreaders.com

Once upon a time there were two children,
a boy called Hansel and his sister, Gretel.
Hansel had short golden hair and Gretel had
long golden hair and they both had big blue
eyes. Hansel and Gretel often played together
and Hansel had a favorite stick that he
sometimes carried.

They lived in a small house near a forest high up on a mountain. Their father was called Hans, and he was a woodcutter. He went to the forest every day and cut wood to sell. He did not make a lot of money and they were a poor family.

Sadly, Hansel and Gretel's mother was dead. She died when they were very little children. Not long ago, their father had married again. Elsa was not a kind woman and she did not like children, especially Hansel and Gretel. But most of all, Elsa did not like being poor.

One night, Elsa said, "We don't have enough food because Hansel and Gretel eat too much! Tomorrow, we must take them far into the forest and lose them. Then we won't have to feed them and we will have enough food!". The children heard these terrible words of Elsa's.

The children were scared and did not know what was going to happen.

But Hansel had an idea.

Later that night, he quietly went out and picked up some white stones. The stones shone brightly in the moonlight. Hansel put the stones in his pockets.

The next day, Elsa told the children to come to the forest to get some wood. Elsa took her basket and set out. She was happy. Hans was not happy. He was sad because he did not want to lose his children, but he was afraid of Elsa.

Gretel was scared.

"Father," she said, "I'm scared. Come with us and hold my hand."

Hans smiled and took Gretel's hand. He wanted to make her feel better.

The family walked into the forest. Elsa went first, then Hans and Gretel, and lastly Hansel who was working on an idea.

Hansel carried out his very good idea as they
walked through the woods.

He dropped white stones on the path
into the forest because he knew that he and
Gretel would find them shining brightly in the
moonlight. The stones would show them how
to get home.

Soon evening came, and the forest got dark.
Hans made a fire.

"We need more wood," said Elsa. "Wait
here children. Your father and I will go and get
some."

Elsa and Hans never came back.

Very quickly, evening turned to night and
the moon came out.

"Look Gretel, the moon is shining on my white stones! We can follow them all the way home," said Hansel.

The children followed the stones until they came out of the forest. Soon they could see their home. They ran to their father and hugged him.

Elsa was angry.

"I hate those children," Elsa thought. "We must try again."

The next day, Elsa gave the children some hard bread for their lunch.

"Let's go and help your father get some more wood," she said.

The children followed Elsa and Hans into the forest again.

Again, Hansel walked behind. This time he dropped pieces of the hard bread onto the path. But as soon as he dropped the pieces of bread, hungry little birds quickly ate them all up. Hansel didn't see this happening.

How were they going to get home, this time?

Evening came. Again Elsa took Hans away and left the children alone beside the fire. When the moon came up, Hansel saw there was no bread to follow home.

They were very upset and scared.

"Come on, we must try to walk home," said Hansel.

The children walked and walked but could not find their way home.

Morning came, and they were tired and hungry.

Suddenly a beautiful bird flew out of a tree.

"Quickly!" said Gretel. "Let's follow it! It might lead us out of the wood to the right path."

The children followed the bird as it flew. It was like a magical bird.

They ran as fast as they could through the forest to keep up with it.

Faster and faster they ran.

Then suddenly, they could not see the bird any more and they stopped.

In front of them, they could see a little house. They had never seen one like it before. It was made of cookies and cake, chocolate, coconut, ice-cream, fruit, sugar, and lots of other sweet things.

"Wow!"

The hungry children quickly ran toward the house. They began to eat.

They were eating the house when an old
woman came out. She was ugly. But she smiled
at them and asked them to eat as much as
they wanted.

"The house won't fall down," she laughed.
Then she said, "Come inside children, come
inside. There's more here."

The children went inside.

The old woman gave them lots of food to eat. They enjoyed it.

"Sleep here tonight," she said. "I'll take you home tomorrow."

"Thank you. You're very kind," said Hansel.

"Thank you very much," said Gretel.

The old woman smiled.

The children went to sleep.

Then suddenly at midnight, the old woman pulled Hansel out of bed!

"Ha!" she shouted. "Now I've got you. I want to eat you!"

The old woman was really a wicked witch and not kind at all.

What were they going to do?

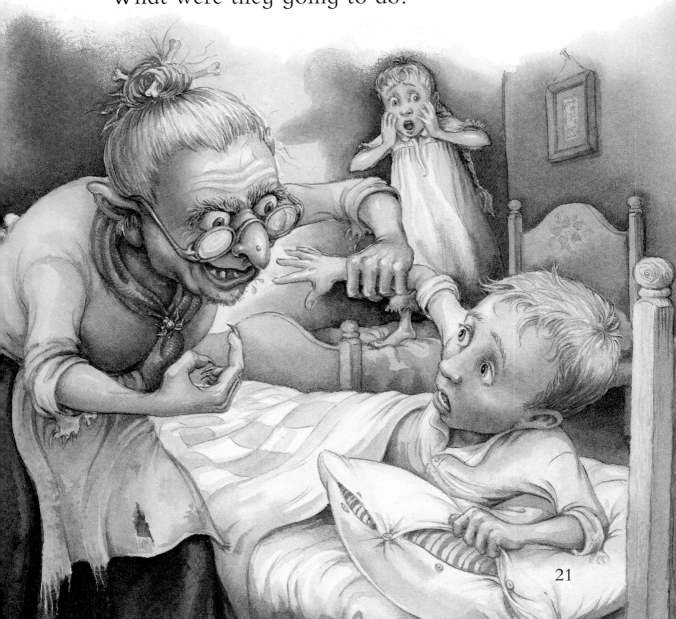

The wicked witch put Hansel in a cage outside. She cooked lots of food for him to eat so he would get fat and be good to eat. She took it out to him.

"Soon I'll eat the boy!" she thought.

"Clean my floor, little one!" she shouted at Gretel.

The witch could not see very well. Every day she asked Hansel, "Are you fat, yet?" because she wanted him fat and juicy to eat.

Clever Hansel always put a chicken bone through the cage for the witch to feel. "Not yet!" she said. "Your finger's too thin."

One day the witch shouted, "I can't wait.
I'll cook the boy today! Little one, put lots of
wood on the fire. I want my oven hot."
Gretel was scared for Hansel. She put wood
on the fire as she was told, while she thought
about what to do.

"Is the fire ready?" the witch asked. She wanted it nice and hot.

Because the witch could not see very well, she bent down to look.

"Get out of my way, girl! I want to see!" the wicked witch shouted at Gretel.

The old witch looked into the big oven.

    Suddenly, Gretel ran behind the witch and pushed her as hard as she could.

    "Aaaaaaaagh!"

    Gretel pushed and pushed until...

The old witch fell into the oven.

    Quickly, Gretel shut the door. Bang! That was the end of the witch.

Gretel ran outside and opened Hansel's cage.

"Hansel! Hansel!" she said. "The wicked witch is dead!"

Hansel came out of his cage.

"Hurry! I know there is treasure, somewhere," said Gretel. "Let's find it and go quickly!"

The children found the treasure and put it in their pockets.

The children ran. It took them a long time to find the way.

At last, far ahead, they could see their house. Their father was working in the garden. They were very excited.

"Father!" they shouted.

He was alone. Where was Elsa?

"Elsa was a bad woman, but she's gone and won't be coming back," their father said.

Hans was happy to see his children again. He thought he had lost them forever.

"I'm sorry I left you in the forest."

Hansel and Gretel told him about the witch and her house.

Then they showed him the treasure they had brought back.

"Look father! Now we're not poor!" said the children.

Hans smiled. "We'll have enough to eat now. But my real treasure is having my two children home again."

From that day, they all lived happily ever after.